◆ CONTEN

◆ Introduction ◆

Collins Amazing People Readers are collections of short stories. Each book presents the life story of five or six people whose lives and achievements have made a difference to our world today. The stories are carefully graded to ensure that you, the reader, will both enjoy and benefit from your reading experience.

You can choose to enjoy the book from start to finish or to dip into your favourite story straight away. Each story is entirely independent.

After every story a short timeline brings together the most important events in each person's life into one short report. The timeline is a useful tool for revision purposes.

Words which are above the required reading level are underlined the first time they appear in each story. All underlined words are defined in the glossary at the back of the book. Levels 1 and 2 take their definitions from the *Collins COBUILD Essential English Dictionary* and levels 3 and 4 from the *Collins COBUILD Advanced English Dictionary.*

To support both teachers and learners, additional materials are available online at www.collinselt.com/readers.

The Amazing People Club®

Collins Amazing People Readers are adaptations of original texts published by The Amazing People Club. The Amazing People Club is an educational publishing house. It was founded in 2006 by educational psychologist and management leader Dr Charles Margerison and publishes books, eBooks, audio books, iBooks and video content, which bring readers 'face to face' with many of the world's most inspiring and influential characters from the fields of art, science, music, politics, medicine and business.

Amazing Scientists

Level 3
CEF B1

Text by
Anne Collins

Series edited by
Fiona MacKenzie

Collins

HarperCollins Publishers
77–85 Fulham Palace Road
Hammersmith London W6 8JB

10 9 8 7 6 5 4 3 2 1

Original text
© The Amazing People Club Ltd

Adapted text
© HarperCollins Publishers Ltd 2014

ISBN: 978-0-00-754510-0

Collins® is a registered trademark of
HarperCollins Publishers Limited

www.collinselt.com

A catalogue record for this book is available
from the British Library

Printed in the UK by Martins the Printers

HarperCollins does not warrant that
www.collinselt.com or any other website
mentioned in this title will be provided
uninterrupted, that any website will be
error free, that defects will be corrected, or
that the website or the server that makes it
available are free of viruses or bugs. For full
terms and conditions please refer to the site
terms provided on the website.

These readers are based on original texts
(BioViews®) published by The Amazing
People Club group.® BioViews® and The
Amazing People Club® are registered
trademarks and represent the views of the
author.

BioViews® are scripted virtual interview
based on research about a person's life and
times. As in any story, the words are only
an interpretation of what the individuals
mentioned in the BioViews® could have
said. Although the interpretations are
based on available research, they do not
purport to represent the actual views of
the people mentioned. The interpretations
are made in good faith, recognizing that
other interpretations could also be made.
The author and publisher disclaim any
responsibility from any action that readers
take regarding the BioViews® for educational
or other purposes. Any use of the BioViews®
materials is the sole responsibility of the
reader and should be supported by their own
independent research.

Cover image © Mrs_ya/Shutterstock

MIX
Paper from
responsible sources
FSC® C007454

◆ THE GRADING SCHEME ◆

The Collins COBUILD Grading Scheme has been created using the most up-to-date language usage information available today. Each level is guided by a brand new comprehensive grammar and vocabulary framework, ensuring that the series will perfectly match readers' abilities.

		CEF band	Pages	Word count	Headwords
Level 1	elementary	A2	64	5,000–8,000	approx. 700
Level 2	pre-intermediate	A2–B1	80	8,000–11,000	approx. 900
Level 3	intermediate	B1	96	11,000–15,000	approx. 1,100
Level 4	upper intermediate	B2	112	15,000–19,000	approx. 1,700

For more information on the Collins COBUILD Grading Scheme, including a full list of the grammar structures found at each level, go to www.collinselt.com/readers/gradingscheme.

Also available online: Make sure that you are reading at the right level by checking your level on our website (www.collinselt.com/readers/levelcheck).

Antoine Lavoisier

◆ ◆ ◆

1743–1794

the man who wrote the first modern
chemistry textbook

I was a French scientist, who people call the <u>founder</u> of modern chemistry. With my wife's help, I wrote the first modern textbook on chemistry. I discovered what water consists of. I died on the <u>guillotine</u> in the French <u>Revolution</u>.

◆ ◆ ◆

I was born in Paris on 26th August 1743 into a family of rich <u>aristocrats</u>. When I was only 5 years old, my mother died, and left me a lot of money. From the age of 11, I went to a very good school, the Collège des Quatre-Nations (also known as the Collège Mazarin), where I studied chemistry, mathematics, <u>astronomy</u> and <u>botany</u>. My father was a lawyer, so my family expected that I'd follow the same profession. But although I studied law, I didn't want to be a lawyer. I was much more interested in science.

In 1766, I wrote an essay with a plan for lighting the streets of Paris. I felt very proud when I received a gold <u>medal</u> from King Louis XV for my essay. I also studied geology, the science of the study of rocks. In 1767, I worked with a team of geologists on a study of the rocks of Alsace-Lorraine.

In 1768, when I was 25, I was elected to the <u>Academy</u> of Sciences, the most important organization for scientists in France. In the same year, I started working in the <u>administration</u> of the Ferme Générale, a private company that collected taxes for the king. The Ferme Générale was hated by the poor <u>peasants</u> of France. Many of the people who collected taxes for the Ferme Générale were very rich, but they didn't earn their money in an honest way. They gave some of the tax money they collected to the King, but they also kept a lot of money for themselves.

I knew this was wrong, and I tried to help the poor peasants. But I'd no idea that one day I'd die because I'd worked for the Ferme Générale.

I was very surprised when one of my work colleagues, an older man called Jacques Paulze, asked me if he could talk to me about his daughter, Marie-Anne. He told me that she lived in a <u>convent</u>. However, a rich and powerful aristocrat called the <u>Count</u> d'Amerval wanted to marry her. But Marie-Anne didn't want to marry the Count, as he was almost 40 and she was only 13. This made the Count very angry. He said that if Marie-Anne didn't marry him, he would remove Jacques from his job at the Ferme Générale.

So Jacques asked me if I'd marry Marie-Anne. If she had a husband already, the Count wouldn't be able to marry her. So I agreed to meet Marie-Anne. I was 28, but in spite of the 15-year difference between our ages, Marie-Anne and I liked each other, so we married on 16ᵗʰ December 1771.

♦ ◆ ♦

Marie-Anne continued her education at the convent, but we met sometimes, and we liked each other more and more. She was very interested in my scientific work, and wanted to learn more about it. After leaving the convent, she began to help me in my work, and for the next twenty years, we worked together as a team.

Marie-Anne had learned English, so she was able to translate the works of English scientists, for example, the chemist, Joseph Priestley. This was very useful for me, as it meant I could learn what scientists in other countries were doing. Marie-Anne was also very good at drawing, and she

Antoine with Marie-Anne

drew excellent diagrams of my experiments. In addition, she helped me write scientific <u>papers</u>, and kept records of my experiments and discoveries.

My work with the Ferme Générale kept me very busy. But in 1775, I was <u>appointed</u> to a new and important job when I became one of four <u>Commissioners</u> of the Royal <u>Gunpowder</u> Administration. There had been some problems with the quality of the gunpowder used in France, but after I started working for the Royal Gunpowder Administration, the quality improved a lot.

My new job was very good for my career as a scientist. I was given a house and a laboratory in the Royal Arsenal, the buildings where the army's equipment was stored. Marie-Anne and I lived and worked there between 1775 and 1792. We often gave parties for other scientists, and they enjoyed visiting us to discuss their work and ideas.

I made many important discoveries about chemistry in my laboratory. I had many questions, and I needed to find answers. One question was, 'What happens when something burns?' One of the main scientific ideas of my time was called the 'phlogiston theory'. According to this theory, or idea, when something burns, a <u>substance</u> called phlogiston is <u>released</u> into the air. But I proved that the gas oxygen is very important when things are burned.

I wasn't the first scientist to discover oxygen but I was the first to call it by this name. Joseph Priestley, an English chemist, and Carl Wilhelm Scheele, a Swedish chemist, had already discovered oxygen at different times, but they called it by other names. In addition, I was the first scientist to prove that oxygen was an <u>element</u>.

◆ ◆ ◆

Scientists of my time believed that water was an element. But I proved that it's a chemical compound, a substance in chemistry that's made up of two or more elements. I discovered that water consists of two elements – oxygen and another gas, hydrogen. I also discovered that air consists mostly of oxygen and the gas nitrogen (although I called this gas azote).

I spent a lot of time separating chemical compounds into elements, and in 1787, I invented a useful system for naming compounds. I also did experiments with breathing. I proved that people breathe in oxygen and breathe out the gas carbon dioxide. I also tried to improve the health of poor people in cities and towns. I believed that people who live in crowded areas need clean air to be healthy.

In 1789, I published an important book about chemistry, which was really the first modern chemistry textbook. Its title was *Traité Élémentaire de Chimie* (Elementary Treatise on Chemistry). It contained a list of elements, and explained how chemical compounds are made from elements, and it also explained the 'laws' of chemistry.

Marie-Anne did thirteen drawings for this book, and it was translated into English by a Scotsman called Robert Kerr. I was very happy and excited about my book, but I didn't know that my happiness was going to end very soon. I didn't know that terrible events were going to happen in France, and that the next few years were going to be very dangerous for aristocrats like me.

For centuries, there had been a huge gap between the rich aristocrats and the poor peasants in France. The peasants had very hard and difficult lives. Unfortunately, most rich people didn't care about the peasants, and they weren't interested in their problems. In addition, they were often cruel to the peasants and, as a result, the peasants became very angry. They blamed the King and the rich aristocrats for all their troubles, and at last they decided it was time to change things.

On 14th July 1789, a huge crowd attacked the Bastille, a great prison in Paris, and <u>released</u> six prisoners inside. This was the start of the French Revolution. During the following years, aristocrats were hunted and arrested by the <u>revolutionaries</u>, and many were killed.

♦ ◆ ♦

I tried to stay away from the revolution, but I couldn't. The revolutionaries hated the Ferme Générale, the organization that I'd worked for. The Ferme Générale had forced the poor peasants to pay heavy taxes, and now the peasants wanted their <u>revenge</u>. So the revolutionaries made a list of all the members of the Ferme Générale, and said that these people were enemies of France. Both my name and the name of Marie-Anne's father were on the revolutionaries' list. I realized that I was in a very dangerous position.

In 1792, I was forced to leave my job on the Gunpowder Commission, and to move from my house and laboratory at the Royal Arsenal. On 24th November 1793, the revolutionaries arrested everyone who had worked for the Ferme Générale, including Marie-Anne's father and me.

Unfortunately, my situation was made even worse because, in the past, I'd made a powerful enemy, a scientist called Jean-Paul Marat. Marat hated me because several years before, he'd applied to become a member of the Academy of Sciences and I'd spoken against him. As a result, the other scientists hadn't accepted him into the Academy.

But later, Marat became a revolutionary leader with a lot of power. He'd waited for years to get his revenge on me, and now at last he had his chance. He accused me of many crimes – for example, stealing money from France, helping foreign scientists and even selling tobacco that had water added to it. Although Marat had been killed in July 1793, before my arrest, the revolutionaries still remembered what he'd said about me.

On 8th May 1794 I was brought to the revolutionary tribunal, the special court of the revolution, and accused of being a traitor to my country, an enemy to France. The judges asked me to defend myself, and I tried to explain that I was a scientist and chemist. Although Marie-Anne and other people said I was an excellent scientist, the judges didn't want to listen. They said that the revolution didn't need scientists or chemists, and I was found guilty, and sentenced to death.

Later that same day, I died on the guillotine, together with Marie-Anne's father, and 27 other people. After my death, the government took away my notebooks and scientific equipment, but Marie-Anne saved as much of my research as she could.

Later, my research was published in a book called *Mémoires de Chimie* (Memories of Chemistry). A year and a half after my death, the government sent my things back to Marie-Anne, with a note that said, 'To the widow of

Lavoisier who was wrongly <u>convicted</u>.' But although the government had admitted they were wrong, and had said that I was innocent, it was too late.

My cruel death hadn't only been terrible for my family and friends, but also for my country, as France had lost a great scientist. It had only taken one moment to cut off my head, but the huge amount of scientific knowledge inside my head was lost for many years. If my life hadn't ended so <u>tragically</u> on that sad day, I could have made many more important discoveries.

The Life of Antoine Lavoisier

1743   Antoine-Laurent Lavoisier was born in Paris, France. He was the son of a lawyer.

1754–1761   He attended the Collège des Quatre-Nations (Collège Mazarin) and became interested in chemistry, botany, science and mathematics.

1762   Antoine trained in law, but didn't become a lawyer.

1763–1767   He studied geology with Jean-Étienne Guettard. He developed a plan for lighting the streets of Paris, and received a gold medal from King Louis XV. In 1767, he worked with Guettard and other geologists on a study of the rocks of Alsace-Lorraine.

1768   At the age of 25, he was elected to the Academy of Sciences. He also worked in the administration of the Ferme Générale, a private company that collected taxes for the King. The following year, Antoine worked on a map which showed the geology of France.

1771   He married Marie-Anne Pierrette Paulze, the daughter of an older colleague in the Ferme Générale.

1772   He started becoming famous as a scientist who always used experiments and facts to prove that his ideas were right.

1774   Antoine met Joseph Priestley, an English
        chemist, in Paris.

1775   He was appointed as a Commissioner of
        the Royal Gunpowder Administration,
        and given a house and a laboratory in
        the Royal Arsenal.

1778   He gave oxygen its name, and published a
        book on <u>acids</u>.

1783   He suggested plans for a new system of
        weights and measures, and published a book,
        Réflexions sur le Phlogistique.

1787   He invented a system for naming chemical
        compounds.

1788   Antoine became worried when his old
        enemy, the scientist Jean-Paul Marat, started
        to become involved in revolutionary politics.

1789   He published the first modern chemistry
        textbook, *Traité Élémentaire de Chimie.* The
        French Revolution began when a crowd
        attacked the Bastille prison on 14th July.

1791   Marat accused Antoine of selling tobacco that
        had water added to it.

1792   Antoine was forced to leave his job with the
        Royal Gunpowder Administration, and move
        out of his house and laboratory.

1793   On 24th November, all members of the Ferme
       Générale were arrested and put in prison,
       including Antoine and Marie-Anne's father.

1794   On 8th May, Antoine was brought to the
       revolutionary tribunal and accused of
       crimes against the people of France. He was
       sentenced to death together with Marie-
       Anne's father and 27 other people, and died
       on the guillotine. Marie-Anne saved as much
       of his research as she could.

Humphry Davy

◆ ◆ ◆

1778–1829

the man who discovered 'laughing gas'

I was a brilliant scientist and chemist. I discovered that 'laughing gas' could stop people feeling pain. I gave popular lectures about science. One of my most famous inventions was the Davy lamp, which improved the safety of <u>coal miners</u>.

♦ ◆ ♦

I was born in the town of Penzance, Cornwall, in the south-west of England, on 17th December 1778. I was the oldest of five children. When I was a boy, I was very interested in science and doing experiments, but I also enjoyed writing poetry and stories. <u>Tragically</u>, the day before my 16th birthday in 1794, my father died from an illness. I had to earn money to help my family.

So in February 1795 I became <u>apprenticed</u> to John Bingham Borlase, a <u>surgeon</u> who also had an excellent knowledge of medicines. During my years as an apprentice, I began studying chemistry, a subject that was going to be very important for my future. I read about the work of famous scientists, including the French scientist Antoine Lavoisier, and I became very interested in his experiments.

My family often had lodgers, people who paid money to live in our house. In June 1797, Gregory Watt, the son of the famous Scottish inventor, James Watt, came to live with us. Gregory had been ill, and his father thought a holiday in Cornwall would help him to get better. The weather in Cornwall is much warmer than in Scotland! So a family friend had suggested that our house in Penzance was a good place for Gregory to stay.

Gregory and I were about the same age, and we were both interested in chemistry and literature. We enjoyed going out together, and having a good time. By the time Gregory left Cornwall in May 1798, we'd become great friends, and we were friends for a long time.

◆ ◆ ◆

I'd started doing experiments with heat and light, and I'd written a letter about my discoveries to Dr Thomas Beddoes. Dr Beddoes was a well-known doctor and scientific writer, who'd started a new institution called the Medical Pneumatic Institution, in the town of Bristol, in the west of England. Its purpose was to find out if gases could make people with diseases feel better.

Dr Beddoes was looking for an assistant to look after his laboratory. A friend had told him about me, and when he read my letter describing my experiments, he was impressed with my work. He thought it was so good that he offered me a job. So in October 1798 I moved to Bristol to be in charge of the laboratory, and soon I was doing interesting experiments on different gases.

One gas I experimented on was nitrous oxide. This was produced by a machine in an underground room of the institution. I discovered that nitrous oxide had a very strange effect on people. When they breathed this gas, they couldn't feel anything, and sometimes they started to laugh. I knew this very well, because it had happened to me too! I didn't have anyone to help me, so I often had to be the subject of my own experiments. When I breathed nitrous oxide, I couldn't stop laughing. Later, this gas became known in many places as 'laughing gas'.

Sometimes my experiments with gases were very dangerous for my health. When I breathed a gas, I sometimes felt great pain and then I had to run from the laboratory into the fresh air.

I started to think about how nitrous oxide could be useful for human beings. In those days, there was no anaesthetic for patients having operations in hospitals, or having work done by dentists. As a result, these poor patients were usually in terrible pain. But if you breathed nitrous oxide, you couldn't feel anything, including pain.

I realized this gas would help people greatly during operations, and I published my research in 1799 in a book called *Researches, Chemical and Philosophical*. But although I suggested that nitrous oxide could be used in operations, unfortunately surgeons and dentists didn't start using it for another 44 years.

Nitrous oxide, also known as 'laughing gas'

1799 was a year of great change for me. A new scientific institution, the Royal Institution, had been started in London by two famous scientists. One was <u>Count</u> Rumford, an inventor who'd married the <u>widow</u> of the famous French chemist, Antoine Lavoisier. The other was Sir Joseph Banks, a <u>naturalist</u> and <u>botanist</u>. He'd sailed with Captain James Cook on his first great voyage to New Zealand and Australia (1768–1771).

Count Rumford and Sir Joseph were looking for a lecturer to give talks at the Royal Institution. They'd heard about me, and were very interested in my work. So in February 1801 they invited me to London for an interview, and offered me a job. This was an important step in my career, so I was very pleased to accept their offer.

I moved to London in March 1801, and on 25th April 1801, I gave my first public lecture at the Royal Institution. I talked about galvanism – electricity produced through the action of chemicals. My first lecture was very successful, so then I gave more lectures which were also very popular.

Many fashionable people in London society started coming to my lectures. I always worked hard to prepare them, and I did a lot of research into my subjects. But I also knew that I had to make my lectures interesting to people who didn't know much about science. So when I could, I gave exciting – and sometimes dangerous! – <u>demonstrations</u> of my experiments, so that people could understand my ideas better.

◆ ◆ ◆

After my lectures on galvanism ended, I gave more lectures on how chemistry is used in farming. My lectures and demonstrations continued to attract a lot of attention. I was very good at talking about scientific subjects in a way that people could understand. In addition, I was young and good-looking, so I was popular with the ladies!

In June 1802, at the age of 23, I became a permanent lecturer at the Royal Institution and a Professor of Chemistry. In November 1804, I became a Fellow (a member) of the Royal Society, an organization of scientists whose purpose was to increase scientific knowledge.

In 1805, the Royal Society gave me the Copley <u>Medal</u> for great achievements in science, and in 1807, I became a <u>founder</u> of the Geological Society. During the following years, I became very famous in the world of science. I did many experiments with chemical substances, and I became one of the first people to work on <u>electrolysis</u>. Through this process, I separated many different chemical <u>elements</u> from each other.

I also spent a lot of time reading about the work of scientists in other countries, for example, the work of Carl Wilhelm Scheele, a Swedish chemist. Scheele had done a lot of work on the chemical substance chlorine, and I continued with this work. In fact, it was me who gave chlorine its name!

In April 1812, two important events happened in my life. On 8th April I married Jane Apreece, a rich widow from Scotland. Three days later, on 11th April, I received a knighthood from King George III. After you receive a knighthood, you can put 'Sir' in front of your name instead of 'Mr', so I became Sir Humphry Davy.

The following year, in October 1813, I left the Royal Institution, and went on a journey to Europe with Jane and my assistant, Michael Faraday. First, we travelled to Paris for an unusual purpose – so that I could receive a medal from the French <u>emperor</u>, Napoleon Bonaparte. France and England were enemies, but although I was English, Napoleon was very impressed by my work as a scientist. He thought it was so good that he gave me the medal.

◆ ◆ ◆

While I was in Paris, I was asked to work on a substance that a French chemist, Bernard Courtois, had discovered. I proved that it was an element, which is now called iodine. I was always interested in the effects that chemicals have on people's health, and later, I did research on iodine for use in medicine and industry.

In December 1813, we left Paris and travelled south to Italy. We stayed in Florence where I did some more chemical experiments with Faraday's help. In June 1814, I met the famous scientist, Alessandro Volta, the inventor of the first battery, in Milan. Next, we visited Switzerland, Austria and Germany. In every country, I met scientists and shared notes and planned experiments with them. Finally we returned to England in 1815.

On my return, I was asked to work on an important new project – to produce a lamp for improving the safety of coal miners. Coal mining was a very dangerous job. Coal miners

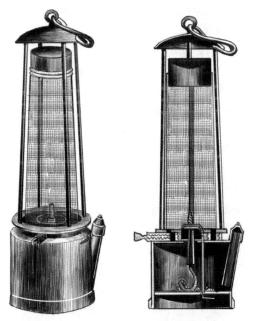

A Davy lamp and section of the inside

had to carry lamps so they could see underground, but these lamps had open flames. There was a dangerous gas called methane in the air underground, and when the flames met this gas, there were terrible explosions. In 1812, there had been a huge explosion in a coal mine near Newcastle in northern England and many men had died.

So I invented a kind of metal <u>gauze</u> that kept the flames inside the lamp so they couldn't spread into the air. The news about my lamp, which was called the Davy lamp, was announced at a meeting of the Royal Society in November 1815. For my work, I was presented with the Rumford Medal in 1816.

My discoveries in chemistry were important in both industry and farming. Owners of businesses and factories realized that science could improve the way that goods were produced. In January 1819, I was made a <u>baronet</u>, the highest <u>honour</u> given to a British scientist, and in 1820, I was elected President of the Royal Society.

However, my health was getting worse, and I was often ill. Perhaps I'd done so many experiments with gases in my life that they'd poisoned me. I'd also damaged my eyes several years earlier in a laboratory explosion. I spent the last years of my life travelling, writing and enjoying my two favourite hobbies – fishing and shooting. In 1829, I died at the age of 50 from heart disease in Geneva, Switzerland, and was buried there.

The Life of Humphry Davy

1778   Humphry Davy was born in Penzance, Cornwall, England.

1788–1793   Humphry attended schools in Penzance and Truro. He was interested both in literature and doing scientific experiments.

1794   Humphry's father died.

1795   He became apprenticed to John Bingham Borlase, a surgeon and pharmacist in Penzance. He wrote some poetry, but later concentrated on science. He began studying chemistry and doing experiments with heat and light.

1797   He met Gregory Watt, son of the famous Scottish inventor, James Watt. The two young men became great friends.

1798   Humphry got a job at the Medical Pneumatic Institution in Bristol as assistant to Dr Thomas Beddoes. He began experiments on nitrous oxide ('laughing gas').

1799   He published details of his work in *Researches, Chemical and Philosophical*.

1801   Humphry was <u>appointed</u> as an Assistant Lecturer at the Royal Institution, London. He gave his first lecture on galvanism, which was very successful.

1802   His lectures became popular, as he included many experiments and demonstrations. At the age of 23, Humphry became a permanent lecturer at the Royal Institution, and also Professor in Chemistry.

1804   Humphry became a Fellow of the Royal Society of London, an important organization of scientists.

1805   He was presented with the Copley Medal by the Royal Society.

1807   He became a founder of the Geological Society. He was the first scientist to do experiments with electrolysis. He named and separated chemical elements.

1808   Humphry continued to name and separate different chemical elements.

1810   He was elected a foreign member of the Royal Swedish Academy of Sciences. He worked on chlorine, and gave it its present name.

1812   Humphry married Jane Apreece, a rich widow. He received a knighthood from King George III, and gave his last lecture at the Royal Institution.

1813   He left the Royal Institution, and with his wife and assistant, Michael Faraday, he travelled to Paris to receive a medal from the French emperor, Napoleon Bonaparte. He also named the element, iodine.

1815   Humphry travelled back to England through Switzerland, Austria and Germany. He invented the Davy lamp, a lamp to improve the safety of coal miners.

1819   Humphry was made a baronet, the highest honour for a British scientist at the time.

1820   He became President of the Royal Society.

1827   He became ill and left his job as President of the Royal Society.

1829   Humphry died, aged 50, from heart disease in Geneva, Switzerland.

Charles Darwin

◆ ◆ ◆

1809–1882

the man who changed people's ideas with his
theory of evolution

I was a great English scientist and <u>naturalist</u>. I went on a five-year expedition and discovered many new things about plants and animals. I wrote a book about the <u>origins</u> of life, which changed the ideas of many people.

◆ ◆ ◆

I was born on 12th February 1809 in the small town of Shrewsbury in England. I was named Charles Robert Darwin, and I was the fifth of six children. My father was a doctor, and my grandfather was a famous <u>botanist</u>.

<u>Tragically</u>, I learned about death when I was still a child, as my mother died when I was only 8. After this, I became very close to my brother Erasmus, who was five years older than me. We were both very interested in science, especially chemistry. In our garden there was a shed – a small building where equipment for the garden was kept. We made this shed into a chemistry laboratory and did many experiments.

This was much more fun than studying Greek and Latin at school!

My father was very keen for me to become a doctor, so in 1825 he arranged for me to study medicine at Edinburgh University in Scotland. But I didn't do very well at my medical studies. I thought that medicine was boring, and I was more interested in plants and animals than people. In addition, I had a big problem as a medical student – I hated the sight of blood!

However, during my time in Edinburgh, I met some very interesting people. One was John Edmonstone, a lecturer in <u>taxidermy</u>, who had a wonderful knowledge of animals. John, who was from Guyana in South America, had been a black slave who'd later been freed. He told me many things about the rainforests of South America, and <u>inspired</u> me to visit them.

In the summer of 1826, I went walking in the mountains in Wales, and wrote notes about the birds and other wildlife there. After I returned to Edinburgh, I joined the Plinian Society, a club for students who were interested in <u>natural history</u>. The members of the Plinian Society wrote <u>papers</u> about natural history, and met every week to present their papers and discuss their ideas.

I became friends with Robert Grant, a scientist who studied animals. He taught me many things about creatures that live in the sea, and we went for walks together, collecting <u>specimens</u> from around the River Forth. I made some discoveries of my own, and in March 1827, I gave a talk about a sea creature to the Plinian Society.

◆ ◆ ◆

I wasn't doing well at my medical studies, so in 1827 I decided to leave Edinburgh University. This made my father very angry, because he thought I was wasting my life. So he sent me to Christ's College, part of Cambridge University, to study <u>theology</u> and become a priest in the Church of England. I studied hard at Cambridge, but I also enjoyed riding, shooting and collecting <u>beetles</u>, a popular hobby at the time.

I became a friend of the <u>Reverend</u> John Stevens Henslow, a professor of <u>botany</u>. Although my real interest was in natural history, I did well in my final theology examinations in January 1831.

My father was keen for me to start work as a priest, but in August 1831, something happened that changed my life. I received a letter from John Henslow about an expedition to South America on a ship called <u>HMS</u> Beagle. This expedition, which was starting four weeks later, was planned to last for two years. Its purpose was to make maps of the coast of South America, but the captain, Captain Robert FitzRoy, was also looking for a scientist or naturalist to go on the expedition. He knew that the voyage would be long and lonely, so he wanted someone who could also be his friend. John Henslow told me that this naturalist wouldn't receive any money, but his job would be very interesting. He could look for new <u>species</u> of plants and animals.

I met Captain FitzRoy, and was very excited when he invited me to go on the expedition. But at first my father refused to let me go. He said that it was a waste of time, and

HMS Beagle

that he wouldn't pay for me. Fortunately, my uncle talked to my father and persuaded him to let me go. After some delay, *HMS Beagle* left England on 27th December 1831. I didn't know that it would be five long years before I saw my home and family again!

I lived in a small cabin – a room on the ship – and I wasn't a good sailor, so I was often <u>seasick</u>. But when I was able to go on land, I collected wonderful specimens of birds, animals, plants and <u>fossils</u>. I wrote notes about everything I found, and I sent my specimens to John Henslow in Cambridge so that he could study them.

◆ ◆ ◆

We sailed to Brazil, where I loved the rainforests, but I was shocked by the terrible system of <u>slavery</u>. We then went south to Patagonia, and stayed for weeks in places where no white person had been before. In 1833, we reached the Falkland Islands, where I found wonderful new animals and plants. We continued our voyage, sailing around Tierra del Fuego at the southern end of South America.

My 25th birthday was on 12th February 1834, and as a birthday present, Captain FitzRoy gave my name to a mountain in Tierra Del Fuego – Mount Darwin. We continued sailing up the coast of Chile, but in August 1834, I became dangerously ill with a fever. After a long time I got better, so we sailed up the coast to Peru and arrived at the Galapagos Islands in September 1835. These islands were wonderful places for learning new things about natural history.

There were no people on the Galapagos Islands, only thousands of animals and birds. As I was studying the wildlife there, I noticed something very interesting. The same species of small bird was living on several of the islands, but on each island, the birds were a little different from each other. And although we'd found the same species of bird on the mainland of South America, those birds were different from the birds on the Galapagos Islands.

In addition, I noticed that there were different kinds of <u>tortoises</u> on the different islands. I realized something very important. Species of animals and birds could adapt themselves to different environments. In other words, a species could change in order to fit better into an environment.

We stayed on the Galapagos Islands for a month, then, in October 1835, we sailed across the Pacific Ocean, arriving in New Zealand in December. From there we went to Sydney in Australia. From Sydney I travelled west to the town of Bathurst and discovered more plants and animals. We continued on to South Africa, stopping at the Cocos Islands and Mauritius on the way. But we'd been travelling for over four years, and we were ready to go home. We finally arrived back in Falmouth, in south-west England, on 2nd October 1836, after a voyage of four years, nine months and five days.

◆ ◆ ◆

Our expedition had ended, but I had many things to think about. I'd found fossils from animals and birds that had lived thousands of millions of years ago. I'd also seen different forms of the same species of animals and birds in different environments. So I started thinking about a new idea.

This was that species of animals and birds change very slowly over hundreds of thousands of years. During this process of slow change, or evolution, only the strongest animals and birds survive. This is because only the strongest ones are able to adapt to new environments. I called this process 'natural selection'. But at first, I didn't want to tell anyone about my idea, because I knew that many people would be angry with me.

Most people in Europe were Christians who believed in the teachings of the Bible, the book of the Christian religion. The Bible said that God created the world and

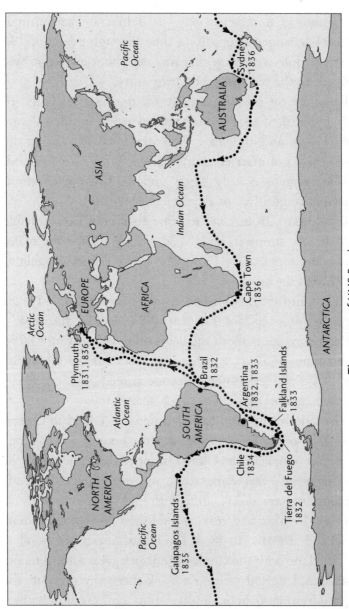

The voyage of HMS Beagle

everything in it in seven days. It didn't say that animals and birds changed over a long time through evolution. So I knew people would say that my idea about evolution was different to the teachings of Christianity.

I worked on my idea quietly for the next 20 years. In 1839, I published an account of our expedition called *Voyage of the Beagle*, and after this, I became very famous. In the same year, I got married to my cousin, Emma Wedgwood. Our marriage was very happy and we had ten children, although, tragically, not all of them survived.

In addition, from time to time I suffered from terrible pains in my stomach, and I had to stay in bed for many weeks. But fortunately, I always got better, and was able to go on with my work.

At last, in 1859, I published my most famous book, *On the Origin of Species by Means of Natural Selection*. In this book, I explained my ideas about the beginnings of life. Only 1,250 copies of my book were printed, and they sold very quickly. But, as I'd expected, not everyone agreed with my ideas, and some people were very much against me.

The Prime Minister, Lord Palmerston, talked to Queen Victoria about a knighthood, a great <u>honour</u> for me, but important people in the Church stopped this. They thought that my ideas were dangerous, and even my old friend, Captain FitzRoy, didn't agree with me!

Over the next few years, I published more books about plants and animals. In 1864, the Royal Society of London presented me with the Copley <u>Medal</u> for great achievements in science. I started writing a book about my own life for my children, and about the life of my famous grandfather, the botanist. But I was often ill, and on 19th April 1882, I died at home, aged 73, with my dear wife and children around me.

After my death, my body was buried in Westminster Abbey in London. I'd become very famous by the time I died. Although not everybody agreed with my ideas, I was respected as a great scientist. Through my work, people learned many new things about the world.

Westminster Abbey

The Life of Charles Darwin

1809   Charles Robert Darwin was born in the town of Shrewsbury in England. His father was a rich doctor and his grandfather was a famous botanist.

1817   Charles's mother died.

1822   Charles and his older brother, Erasmus, made a chemistry laboratory in their garden shed, where they learned about science and did experiments.

1825–1827   Charles spent two years studying medicine at Edinburgh University. He became friends with John Edmonstone, who taught Charles about taxidermy. He joined the Plinian Society and gave his first talk in March 1827.

1828   Charles was sent to Christ's College, Cambridge University, to study theology. He met the Reverend John Stevens Henslow, Professor of Botany.

1831   Charles was invited by Captain Robert FitzRoy to join the *HMS Beagle* expedition to South America. The expedition set sail on 27th December.

1832–1833   Charles discovered some important fossils in Patagonia, South America. He also discovered many new plants and animals on the Falkland Islands.

1834   *HMS Beagle* sailed around Tierra del Fuego to the Pacific Ocean, then up the coast of Chile. Charles became dangerously ill with a fever, but got better. *HMS Beagle* continued sailing up the coast to Peru.

1835   Charles studied the natural history of the Galapagos Islands and began thinking about the idea of the evolution of species.

1836   The expedition sailed to New Zealand and Australia, arriving in Sydney Harbour on 12th January. *HMS Beagle* finally sailed for England. On the way, it visited the Cocos Islands, Mauritius, South Africa and South America. It arrived in Falmouth, Cornwall on 2nd October.

1837   Charles was elected to the Council of the Geological Society. He met his cousin, Emma Wedgwood.

1838–1839   He started to develop his ideas about natural selection.

1839   Charles and Emma married. They moved to London and later had ten children. Charles published *The Journal of a Naturalist* and was elected a Fellow of the Royal Society, an important organization of scientists. He published *Zoology of the Voyage of HMS Beagle*.

1842–1846   The Darwins moved to Down House
             in Bromley, Kent, south-east England.
             Charles wrote an essay about evolution. He
             published several papers about the places he
             had visited during *HMS Beagle's* voyage.

1848   Charles's father, Robert, died.

1851   Charles and Emma's oldest daughter, Annie,
        died, aged ten.

1853   Charles was presented with the Royal Medal
        by the Royal Society.

1854–1856   He continued reading and doing
             experiments. He started work on his
             book *On the Origin of Species*, in which he
             explained his ideas about evolution by natural
             selection.

1859   1,250 copies of *On the Origin of Species* were
        published, and quickly sold. The Prime
        Minister, Lord Palmerston, wanted Charles
        to receive a knighthood, but the Church
        stopped this.

1862   Charles published *Fertilization of Orchids*, a
        book about an unusual and beautiful flower
        which grew on the Darwins' land.

1864   The Royal Society presented Charles with
        the Copley Medal.

1865–1879   Charles published several more books about plants and animals. *The Descent of Man* was published in 1871. He also began writing the story of his own life for his children.

1879–1881   He published a book about the life of his famous grandfather.

1882   Charles died, aged 73, at home with his family. He was buried in Westminster Abbey, London.

Gregor Mendel

◆ ◆ ◆

1822–1884

the man who first discovered the science of genetics

I was the <u>founder</u> of <u>genetics</u>, but I wasn't famous as a scientist during my life. I was a <u>monk</u> who loved nature and plants. I experimented with pea plants and found the key to one of life's great mysteries.

◆ ◆ ◆

I was born on 20th July 1822, in the town of Heinzendorf. At that time, Heinzendorf was part of the Austrian Empire, but today it's called Hyncice and is in the Czech Republic. My parents, Anton and Rosine, were farmers. They named me Johann, but later I changed my name to Gregor. I had two sisters, and we all lived and worked together on our farm, which had belonged to our family for about 130 years. I loved nature, and I was very interested in learning about the plants and animals on the farm. There were many honey bees in our area too. As a child, I studied how to look after bees, and I also worked as a gardener.

But I also studied hard at school. When I was 11, one of my teachers told my parents that I was very intelligent and worked very hard. He advised them to send me to a secondary school in the town of Troppau (now known as Opava), where I could receive a good education. It wasn't easy for my family to send me to this school, because they didn't have much money, and the school was very expensive. But I did well there, and in 1840, I graduated with great <u>honours</u>.

After this, I applied to study at the University of Olmütz, and was delighted when I was accepted. I studied physics, maths and philosophy, and again I did very well in my studies, and graduated in 1843.

My family expected that I'd become a farmer, but I wanted to continue with my education. However, I knew that my parents couldn't afford to pay for further study, so I found a way to go on with my education for free – by becoming a monk! I joined the Augustinian order, a special group of monks, in the St Thomas <u>monastery</u> in Brno, and I changed my name from Johann to Gregor. I knew that I'd have to work very hard at the monastery, but I didn't mind that, because it had excellent facilities for learning. It was a centre of culture for the area, and it had a wonderful library, where I could do research.

◆ ◆ ◆

Although I enjoyed life at the monastery, I found it very hard, and sometimes I became ill. Some of my duties involved working with the people who lived in the area around the monastery. I was sent to a school to do some teaching work, and the following year, I took a teaching exam, but unfortunately I failed it.

In 1851, the monastery paid for me to attend the University of Vienna, where I studied physics and chemistry. In addition, I studied zoology, the science of the study of animals, and botany. This was a wonderful chance for me, as I was taught by famous scientists, for example, Christian Doppler and Frank Unger, who both inspired me greatly.

In addition, I learned some important things about mathematics. I learned how to design experiments and analyse data, using statistical methods in order to understand the data fully. Later, when I started my experiments, I found that this knowledge was very useful.

In 1853, I completed my university studies and returned to the monastery at Brno. The Abbot, the head of the monastery, then sent me to a school to teach science. I stayed in this job for the next ten years, teaching secondary school pupils. At the same time, I lived in the monastery and began doing experiments. I didn't know that I was going to be famous in the future because of these experiments.

◆ ◆ ◆

I'd always loved plants, and spending time in the peaceful garden of the monastery. As I worked quietly in the garden, looking after the plants, I became very curious about them. I was especially interested in the way that plants reproduced, so I decided to do some experiments to find out more about this. I chose pea plants as the subjects of my experiments, because there were over twenty different kinds of pea plant, so I could get very detailed results.

Between 1856 and 1863, I did a huge number of experiments. I tested about 29,000 pea plants and recorded the results. I concentrated on seven different traits of the plants.

I chose plants with traits that were 'opposite' to each other – for example, plants that were tall or short, plants with round seeds or curved seeds, plants with green peas or yellow peas, and plants that produced peas with smooth or wrinkled skins. I discovered that when I cross-bred plants that produced smooth peas with plants that produced wrinkled peas, all the new plants they produced had peas with smooth skins. These new plants were hybrid plants – in other words, a mixture of two different kinds of plants.

But when I cross-bred these hybrid plants with other plants, they produced some plants with peas with wrinkled skins. In other words, in the first generation of plants, the peas all had smooth skins, but in the second generation, some peas had wrinkled skins.

I was very excited by the results of my experiment, but I needed to find out more. So I did another experiment, and this time I cross-bred thousands of pea plants that had round seeds with pea plants that had curved seeds. The new hybrid plants that were produced all had round seeds. But when I cross-bred these hybrid plants with other pea plants, the results were very interesting.

Because of my training in mathematics from the University of Vienna, I was able to analyse the results using statistical methods. I found that 5,474 plants of this second generation of pea plants had round seeds, and 1,850 plants had curved seeds. In other words, there was a ratio of almost exactly 3:1.

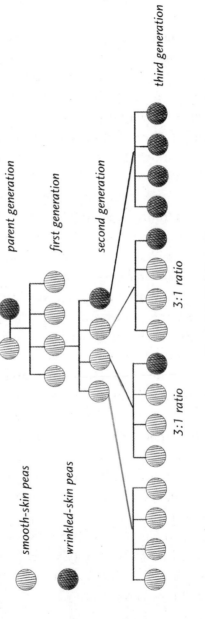

smooth-skin peas

wrinkled-skin peas

parent generation

first generation

second generation

third generation

3:1 ratio

3:1 ratio

Mendel's table of heredity

57

♦ ◆ ♦

I realized there was a pattern in the way the traits of the pea plants were passed on from generation to generation. When pea plants with different traits reproduced with each other, their traits didn't mix together. In my first experiment, each hybrid plant was carrying both 'smooth' and 'wrinkled' traits, but only the 'smooth' trait could be seen. The 'wrinkled' trait was there too, but it was invisible and could not be seen.

In my second experiment, each hybrid plant was carrying both 'round seed' and 'curved seed' traits but only the 'round seed' trait could be seen. But although some traits were invisible in the first generation of pea plants, they appeared in later generations.

I became convinced that my discovery could be applied to all living things, not just plants. I thought about it for a long time, then I wrote down two 'laws' about heredity. According to my first law – the Law of Segregation – the traits of parents don't mix in their children. They are passed as separate traits from generation to generation.

My second law – the Law of Independent Assortment – proved that traits aren't linked to each other, and don't depend on each other. For example, blue eyes and black hair. A person with blue eyes doesn't *always* have black hair – their hair can be brown, red or any other colour.

I knew that my discovery was important, and I tried to tell people about my work, but unfortunately only a few people learned about me. Famous scientists such as the great English scientist, Charles Darwin, who lived at the same time, didn't know about me.

In 1865, I gave two lectures to the <u>Natural History</u> Society of Brno, and I presented a <u>paper</u>, *Experiments with Plant Hybrids*. In this paper, I described how traits were passed on from generation to generation. The following year, my paper was published, although it wasn't read by many people at the time. However, many years later it was <u>acknowledged</u> as one of the most important publications in the history of science.

◆ ◆ ◆

After completing my work with plants, I started doing experiments on honey bees. I <u>bred</u> the bees in <u>beehives</u> that I'd designed myself, and I studied the ways that they reproduced. Sometimes this wasn't pleasant, because the bees didn't want to be studied, so they often <u>stung</u> me! In addition, I did experiments with a plant called hawkweed, which I was hoping would show the same results as my work with peas. Unfortunately, I failed, not because my ideas were wrong, but because I didn't know that hawkweed has a very unusual kind of <u>genetic</u> pattern.

I had other interests too. One was meteorology, the study of the weather. For 27 years, I'd kept records every day of wind speed, wind direction and the amount of rain that fell.

In 1868, I was elected Abbot of the monastery, and after this, my work in science mostly came to an end. Not only was I very busy with the duties of my new job, but I couldn't see as well as before. As a result, it was very difficult for me to continue working on my experiments. So I became very involved with things going on at the monastery.

In 1874, I became involved in a long argument with the government about taxes. The government had a plan to tax religious organizations like the monastery. I was very much against this plan, and I did everything I could to stop it. On 6th January 1884, I died, aged 61, in Brno, and my body was buried at the monastery.

Unfortunately, my notebooks with information about my experiments were destroyed by the monks. Like many people, they didn't understand how important my discoveries were. A few months before my death, I wrote, 'I am convinced that it will not be long before the whole world acknowledges the results of my work'. I was right!

However, this didn't happen until 15 years later when other scientists discovered the same things as I had. Many important things have been learned as a result of my work, for example, how diseases can be passed on from generation to generation, and how the <u>genes</u> of plants can be changed. I am often called 'the father of genetics' because my discoveries about genetics showed the way for other scientists to follow.

The Life of Gregor Mendel

1822   Mendel was born in Heizendorf in the
Austrian Empire. His parents named him
Johann. At the age of 11, he was sent to
secondary school in Troppau (now Opava).
He studied how to look after bees, and
worked as a gardener.

1840–1843   He attended the Philosophical Institute of
the University of Olmütz, where he studied
physics, maths and philosophy. He graduated
in 1843.

1843   Aged 21, he began training as a monk.
He entered the Augustinian Abbey of
St Thomas in Brno, and changed his name
to Gregor.

1846–1847   He studied farming at the Institute of
Philosophy in Brno.

1851   He entered the University of Vienna and
studied physics, chemistry, zoology and
botany. In addition, he studied mathematics.

1853   He returned to the abbey, and was sent to
teach science in a secondary school. This job
lasted for the next ten years.

1856–1863   Gregor tested around 29,000 pea plants at
the monastery. He recorded and analysed the
results using statistical methods.

1865 After his discoveries about genetic traits in pea plants, Gregor created two laws: The Law of Segregation and the Law of Independent Assortment (Mendel's Laws of Inheritance). He presented a paper, *Experiments with Plant Hybrids*, to the Natural History Society of Brno. He started a society in Austria for people interested in meteorology, and he began doing experiments on bees.

1866 His paper was published in the *Proceedings of the Natural History Society of Brno.*

1868 Gregor was elected to the position of Abbot at the monastery.

1870 He published the results of his experiments on hawkweed.

1872 Gregor was given an award – the Cross of the Royal and Imperial Order of Franz Josef I.

1874 He became involved in an argument with the government about taxes on religious organizations.

1876–1881 The Government tried to stop his arguments about the tax law. They <u>appointed</u> him as Vice-Governor, then Governor, of the Moravian Mortgage Bank.

1884 Gregor died at the age of 61 in Brno.

Louis Pasteur

◆ ◆ ◆

1822–1895

the man who saved millions of lives by killing germs

I was a famous French scientist. I proved that many diseases are spread by <u>germs</u> carried in the air. I invented ways to kill germs, and developed <u>vaccines</u> against diseases. I saved the lives of millions of people and animals.

◆ ◆ ◆

I was born on 27th December 1822 in the town of Dole in the eastern part of France, and grew up in the nearby town of Arbois. As a child, I was very good at drawing and painting, and did many drawings of my parents and friends. In 1838, I was sent away to school in Paris, but I missed my home and family, so I returned to Arbois. The following year, I began studying at the Collège Royal in Besançon, a town nearer to my home than Paris. In 1840, I received a <u>Bachelor of Arts</u> degree and started working as a teacher's assistant. Two years later, I received a <u>Bachelor of Science</u> degree from Dijon.

My career began well when, in 1846, I was <u>appointed</u> as Professor of Physics at the College of Tournon. In 1848, I was appointed as Professor of Physics at the Lycée of Dijon, and in the same year, I was appointed as Professor of Chemistry at Strasbourg University. Here I met and fell in love with Marie Laurent, the daughter of the head of the university. We married in 1849, and later had five children, although <u>tragically</u>, three of them died from illnesses. I taught and did research at Dijon and Strasbourg for several years. Then in 1854, I was appointed as Professor of Chemistry and Dean of the Science <u>Faculty</u> at the University of Lille.

The Science Faculty of the university was very active in helping and supporting local industries. If an industry had a problem, they asked the Science Faculty to try and find a solution. At that time, Lille was the most important place in France where drinks like beer were produced.

In 1856, the father of one of my students, a man called Bigo, came to ask for my help. Bigo owned a factory that made drinks, but he was very worried about the beer that the factory produced. A lot of beer was becoming sour, and had to be thrown away because people couldn't drink it. Bigo was losing money because he couldn't sell the bad beer, and he asked me to find out why the beer was turning sour.

I examined some of the sour beer and found that it contained thousands of microbes. I was convinced that these microbes, or germs, were the reason that the beer was becoming sour. But where did the microbes come from and how did they get into the beer? My idea was that they were carried in the air.

Over the next few years, I did many experiments to prove that I was right. I also found that the same thing happened with milk – milk became sour because of tiny microbes. I did more work, and discovered a new process. During this process, germs were removed by boiling wine, beer or milk and then cooling it. Later, this process was called by my name – pasteurization – and it's still used all over the world.

◆ ◆ ◆

I knew that my discovery about germs was very important. Many people and animals died from diseases, and I was sure that these diseases happened because of germs. I was also sure that people became ill because germs were carried through the air from one person to another.

But other scientists didn't agree with my ideas. They thought that germs grew and developed by themselves *inside* the body of a living creature, and they didn't believe that germs could attack a person's body from *outside*. In addition, they didn't believe that a tiny thing like a germ could kill a large human being or animal. So I had to prove that my ideas were right. I gave several presentations about my work, and in 1860, I published an important <u>paper</u> about my research.

In April 1864, I presented my work on pasteurization at a meeting of famous scientists at the University of Paris, and finally, the French Academy of Scientists accepted my ideas. In 1865, I became the Director of Scientific Studies at the École Normale. Then I made another great step forwards.

The silk industry, in the South of France, was losing money because many of the <u>silkworms</u> were dying from a strange disease. This was a very serious problem, as the silk factories were in danger of closing. This meant that the silk workers would lose their jobs and the owners of the factories would lose a lot of money. So they asked me to try and find out why the silkworms were dying.

I moved south to the city of Arles, the centre of the silk industry, and over the next few years, I did a lot of research and experiments on the silkworms. I found that the reason for the silkworm disease was microbes, which were attacking healthy silkworm eggs. So if I could destroy these microbes, the disease would end too. I did more research, and finally I discovered a process to destroy the microbes. So I was able to help save the French silk industry, and everyone was very happy with my work.

In 1868, something terrible happened to me. I became ill with a serious brain disease. After a long time, I got better, but as a result, I could no longer move part of my body. Fortunately, I was still able to continue with my research. I started working on vaccines as a way of preventing diseases in people and animals.

The idea of vaccines wasn't new. In 1796, an English doctor called Edward Jenner had invented a vaccine for smallpox, a terrible disease. He'd carried out his first experiment in the same year, and this had been very successful. But there was still a lot more work to be done. Many chicken farmers in France had serious problems because their chickens were dying from a disease called chicken cholera. So my team of scientists and I started working on a vaccine to prevent this disease.

In 1880, I made a very important discovery about chicken cholera, but it happened by mistake! As part of an experiment, a member of my team, Charles Chamberland, injected a group of chickens with a special mixture containing chicken cholera germs. But he used the wrong mixture. Instead of a mixture with fresh cholera germs, he used a mixture with old germs. So I told Charles to inject the chickens with the fresh mixture.

We expected that the chickens would become ill from cholera and die, but they didn't. So I realized that the chickens had become immune to cholera – in other words, they were protected from cholera because their bodies already contained a weak form of the disease. We'd discovered a vaccine for chicken cholera!

I was very excited about our discovery, and for the next few years my team and I continued working on vaccines. In 1881, we developed a vaccine for anthrax, a disease of cows, sheep and other animals. However, some other scientists didn't believe that my vaccine would work, so I decided to give them a public demonstration.

In 1882, I injected a large number of sheep, cows and goats with anthrax germs. Some of these animals had already been injected with my anthrax vaccine, and these animals survived and were very healthy. But the animals which hadn't been injected with the vaccine became ill and died. Now everyone could see that my vaccine really worked, and they were very impressed. They thought that my work was excellent.

◆ ◆ ◆

My work on germs <u>inspired</u> doctors and other scientists to find safe ways to work with sick people. Many doctors in hospitals and their assistants didn't understand that it was important to keep places clean. They didn't understand that germs could spread from one person to another. So they didn't wash their hands before touching sick people, and they didn't clean their medical equipment. They didn't wear clean clothes, or cover their hair or their faces during operations. As a result, about half the people who had successful operations died from <u>infection</u>. One of my friends was the famous English doctor, Joseph Lister. We worked together to make people understand that it was important to keep hospitals clean.

I continued for many years developing vaccines to prevent people getting diseases. My colleague, Émile Roux, had developed a vaccine for rabies, a terrible disease that you can get if you're bitten by an <u>infected</u> dog. A person with rabies usually dies a painful and terrible death. We'd been working on the vaccine for a long time, and had successfully tested it on eleven dogs.

However, on 6th July 1885, a nine-year-old boy, Joseph Meister, was brought to me. Poor little Joseph had been bitten by a dog infected with rabies. I had a very difficult decision to make. We'd never tried our rabies vaccine on a human being, and I really didn't know if it would work. But I knew that if I didn't give it to Joseph, he was going to die. So I injected him with the vaccine, and three months later he was completely better! I was very happy about that.

The Pasteur Institute

When people heard about my success with the rabies vaccine, I became very famous and I received many awards for my work. People gave money to build the Pasteur Institute in Paris, for research on diseases and their treatment. The Institute was opened on 14th November 1888, and I was appointed as its director. Many important medical discoveries have happened there, and since 1908, several scientists from the Pasteur Institute have won the <u>Nobel Prize</u>.

By the time I died on 28th September 1895, I was a national hero in France. I received <u>honours</u> from my country because I'd saved the lives of millions of human beings and animals.

The Life of Louis Pasteur

1822 Louis Pasteur was born in Dole, in the eastern part of France. He grew up in the town of Arbois.

1837 By the age of 15, Louis was a talented artist. Later, his drawings were kept in the museum of the Pasteur Institute, in Paris.

1838 Louis attended the Institution Barbet, a school in Paris. The following year, he attended the Collège Royal in Besançon.

1840 He received his Bachelor of Arts Degree and began working as a teacher's assistant at Besançon. He also studied mathematics.

1842 Louis received his Bachelor of Science Degree at Dijon.

1846 He was appointed as Professor of Physics at the College of Tournon.

1848 Louis was appointed as Professor of Physics at the Lycée of Dijon. He was also appointed as acting Professor of Chemistry, at Strasbourg University. Here he met Marie Laurent, the daughter of the head of the university.

1849   Louis and Marie married. They later had
        five children, but tragically, only two
        survived.

1852   He was appointed to the Chair of
        Chemistry, the Head of the Department
        of Chemistry, in the Faculty of Science at
        Strasbourg University.

1854   Louis became Professor of Chemistry and
        Dean at the Faculty of Science at Lille
        University.

1856   The Royal Society of London, an important
        organization of scientists, presented him
        with the Rumford <u>Medal</u>. Louis became
        Administrator and Director of Scientific
        Studies at the École Normale Supérieure,
        in Paris.

1857   He presented his research on why milk and
        other liquids become sour.

1860   Louis published a paper on why milk and
        other liquids turn sour.

1862   He presented his first completed test on
        pasteurization.

1865   He did experiments on silkworms and
        discovered why they were dying from a
        disease. After more research, he found a
        way to destroy the disease.

1868   Louis became seriously ill, and got better, but he could no longer move all of his body. During the following years, he studied ways of preventing diseases through vaccines.

1873   Louis was elected to the Académie de Medicine and made Commander in the Brazilian Order of the Rose. In 1874, he was presented with the Copley Medal by the Royal Society of London.

1880   He discovered a vaccine for chicken cholera. This was followed by the development of vaccines for serious diseases in humans.

1881   He developed a vaccine for anthrax. A year later, after a successful public demonstration of the vaccine, he was accepted into the French Academy of Scientists.

1885   Louis developed a vaccine for rabies, and successfully used it on Joseph Meister, a 9-year-old boy.

1888   The Pasteur Institute in Paris was opened on 14th November.

1895   Louis won the Leeuwenhoek Medal, the highest Dutch honour in Arts and Sciences. He died at the age of 72, in Marnes-la-Coquette, Hauts-de-Seine, France.

Francis Crick

• ♦ •

1916–2004

the man who helped to discover the structure of DNA

I was a British scientist. I worked with James Watson and helped to discover the <u>structure</u> of <u>DNA</u>, one of the most important discoveries of the twentieth century. In 1962, James and I won a <u>Nobel Prize</u> with another scientist, Maurice Wilkins.

♦ ◆ ♦

I was born on 8th June 1916 in the village of Weston Favell, Northamptonshire, England, and was named Francis Harry Compton Crick. My father and uncle owned a boot and shoe factory. I went to school first at Northampton Grammar School, then later at Mill Hill School, London. As a child, I was very curious and I was always asking questions. I was very interested in science and I loved physics and chemistry, and doing scientific experiments at home.

My love of science came from my family. My grandfather was very interested in <u>natural history</u>, and he'd written letters to Charles Darwin, the famous scientist. I told my mother that I had one big worry – I was afraid that by the time I grew up, there would be nothing left in the world for me to discover!

I studied physics at University College, London, and graduated in 1937. I began research for a <u>PhD</u>, but in 1939 the Second World War started, so I had to give up my studies. During the war, I worked as a research scientist for the British Admiralty, the government department in charge of the Navy. I worked on designing bombs for war at sea.

In 1940, I married my first wife, Ruth Dodd, and we had a son, Michael. After the war ended in 1945, I continued working for the Admiralty. Then I read a book by Erwin Schrödinger, an Austrian scientist who won the Nobel Prize in Physics in 1933. Schrödinger was very interested in the idea of using physics in the study of biology, especially the study of <u>genes</u>. I found his ideas very exciting.

I already knew a lot about physics, but now I decided to study biology. In 1947, I left the Admiralty. I was given a grant, an amount of money, by the Medical Research Council (MRC), and I started working at the Strangeways Research Laboratory in Cambridge. I had many things to learn about my new subject – it almost felt like being born again!

There was another big change in my life too. In 1947, after seven years, my marriage to Ruth ended. Two years later, in 1949, I married my second wife, Odile. Later, Odile and I had two daughters, Gabrielle Anne and Jacqueline Marie-Thérèse. In the same year, I started working on an MRC project at the Cavendish Laboratory, Cambridge University.

♦ ◆ ♦

The following year, in 1950, I began doing research for a PhD with Gonville and Caius College, Cambridge. But in 1951, I met a young man who was going to change my life. He was an American science student called James Watson who joined the MRC project, and came to share my office. I was 35, and James was only 23, but in spite of the 12 year difference in our ages, we became good friends and colleagues.

Both of us were very interested in DNA (deoxyribonucleic <u>acid</u>) and we shared a passion, a very strong interest, for finding out more about it. We spent many hours discussing our ideas about DNA, and more than anything, we wanted to find out its structure. Although we knew that <u>genetic</u> information was stored in DNA, we wanted to find out how.

DNA is a chemical which is essential to life, and is present in every <u>cell</u> of the body. It's like a genetic 'blueprint' of the body — it carries all the information about how a living creature looks and behaves. We knew we weren't the only scientists doing research into DNA. Two other MRC biochemists, scientists who study chemical processes in living things, were also working on it. Their names were Rosalind Franklin and Maurice Wilkins, and they'd already found out a lot of information at their laboratory in King's College, London. Rosalind Franklin had also taken some important photographs. So James and I were very lucky, because we were able to use the data that Rosalind and Maurice had already collected.

James and I continued working for many months, then one morning in February 1953, we had an amazing breakthrough, a great moment when we achieved our goal. We finally succeeded in discovering the structure of DNA. We were very happy and excited, because we knew that our discovery was of huge importance to science. Many things in the world were going to change because of it. So at lunchtime, we went out to a pub in Cambridge to celebrate. This pub was called *The Eagle*, and it was near the Cavendish Laboratory, where we worked. *The Eagle* was popular with scientists from the Cavendish, and they often went there to relax over lunch, and discuss their ideas.

On 28th February 1953, James and I walked into *The Eagle* for lunch as usual. But then I did something which was very strange. I announced in a loud voice that we'd found 'the secret of life'. All the other customers stopped eating and looked at me in great surprise, but it was true! We really *had* found the secret of life!

We'd discovered exactly how DNA stores genetic information and how it replicates itself – in other words, how DNA makes copies of itself. We'd answered the question, 'How do living things reproduce themselves?' We'd found the key to a whole new world of science, and opened the door to a new understanding of genetics.

◆ ◆ ◆

After that day, *The Eagle* became very famous. If you visit Cambridge today, you can see a large blue notice on the wall. This notice was unveiled by James Watson in a special ceremony in 2003, when he was 75 years old. At the top, it says, 'DNA Double Helix 1953 – The secret of life.' Under this, it says, 'It was here on 28/2/53 that Francis

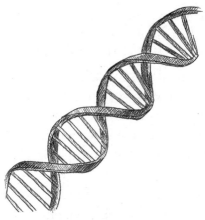

A double helix

Crick and James Watson first announced their discovery of how DNA carries genetic information.'

The 'double helix' was the name that we gave to the structure of DNA. It's formed by two thin pieces of DNA <u>twisted</u> into a <u>spiral</u> shape, like a <u>curved</u> ladder. Since our discovery, the shape of DNA has become very well known.

On 25th April 1953, we published the news of our discovery in a British scientific <u>journal</u> called *Nature*. Since then, many important changes have happened because of what we found out about DNA. For example, in medicine, scientists have been able to create new drugs and <u>vaccines</u>. They can also change the genes of plants to prevent them from getting diseases. As each person's DNA is <u>unique</u>, DNA can be used to identify people.

In the mid-1980s, Alec Jeffreys developed <u>DNA fingerprinting</u> methods. <u>Forensic</u> scientists use DNA found in blood, skin, hair and <u>saliva</u> to identify people who've committed crimes, even crimes long ago. DNA can also be used to identify victims of accidents, crimes and natural disasters, and the parents of children.

In 1962, James, Maurice Wilkins and I received the Nobel Prize in Medicine. But <u>tragically</u>, Rosalind Franklin, who had also done so much work on DNA, had died in 1958, aged just 37. Many people felt very sorry about this, and said that Rosalind also deserved to win the Nobel Prize. But unfortunately, the Nobel Prize can't be given to someone after their death.

I knew that James and I couldn't have succeeded without the work of Rosalind and other scientists. We'd discovered the structure of DNA in February 1953, but Rosalind and the others were also very close to discovering it too. James and I were lucky because we were the ones to discover it, but if we hadn't, I'm convinced that other scientists would have discovered it very soon.

◆ ◆ ◆

After our great discovery, I named my home in Cambridge 'Golden Helix', like the double helix of DNA. I continued to study DNA and in 1954, I completed my PhD, and went to Brooklyn Polytechnic Institute, New York, to do research in the laboratory there. Two years later, I returned to the UK, and in 1962, I became the Director of the Laboratory of <u>Molecular</u> Biology at Cambridge University.

In 1966, I wrote a book called *Of Molecules and Men*, about all the important discoveries that had been made by biochemists, and the changes that had happened. In 1969, I wrote about the future of science in *Nature*, the same journal that had published our discovery about DNA in 1953.

I received many important scientific awards, and in 1976 I went to California to do research at the Salk Institute for Biological Studies in San Diego. In 1977, I moved permanently to California, where I lived for the rest of my life, although I was still a British citizen. I became very interested in and excited by <u>neuroscience</u>. So I did a lot of research into the brain, the mind, and the purpose of dreams.

In 1981, I wrote a book called *Life Itself: Its <u>Origin</u> and Nature*. This book contained some very unusual ideas, but not everybody agreed with them and some people even thought I was crazy! For example, I suggested that the <u>seeds</u> for life on Earth may have been brought to Earth from another planet.

Between 1990 and 2004, I wrote many articles, and in 1991, I was given the Order of Merit, a very special <u>honour</u>, by the British Queen, Elizabeth II. In 1998, I wrote a book about the story of my own life, but I never liked public attention, or giving interviews about myself.

Many things have been given my name. In 2003, the Francis Crick Lecture was started, a chance for young scientists every year to present their work and win a prize.

I died in July 2004, aged 88, in San Diego, California, USA, but I'll never be forgotten. I hope that future generations will continue to use their knowledge of DNA to help human beings.

The Life of Francis Crick

1916   Francis Harry Compton Crick was born in Weston Favell, England. His family had a boot and shoe factory.

1928   At the age of 12, Francis stopped wanting to go to church as he preferred scientific research to religion.

1931   He left Northampton Grammar School and attended Mill Hill School, in London. He studied mathematics, physics and chemistry.

1937   He graduated from University College, in London, with a <u>Bachelor of Science</u> degree in physics.

1938   He began working for a PhD in physics. He did research in the laboratory of Edward Neville da Costa Andrade, at University College.

1939–1945   The Second World War began. At one time, a bomb fell through the roof of the laboratory where Francis was working, and destroyed his experiments. During the war years, he worked for the Admiralty Research Laboratory on designs of mines.

1940   Francis married Ruth Doreen Dodd. They had a son, Michael.

1947   Francis began studying biology instead of physics. He worked on a biology project at Cambridge's Strangeways Laboratory. His marriage to Ruth ended.

1949   He married Odile Speed. Francis started working on a Medical Research Council project at Cavendish Laboratory, Cambridge University. He started studying the structure of DNA.

1950   Francis began a PhD with Gonville and Caius College, Cambridge.

1951   Francis and Odile had a daughter, Gabrielle Anne. He met James Watson and began working with him to discover the structure of DNA.

1952   Using data from Rosalind Franklin and Maurice Wilkins, Francis and James continued work on the structure of DNA.

1953   Francis and James discovered that the structure of DNA was a double helix. They published the news of their discovery in the scientific journal, *Nature*.

1954   Francis and Odile had their second daughter, Jacqueline Marie-Thérèse. Francis completed his PhD. He continued working on molecular biology in the laboratory at Brooklyn Polytechnic Institute, New York.

1956   He returned to England and did more research with James Watson in Cambridge.

1960   Francis was made a Fellow of Churchill College, Cambridge, and University College, London.

1962   Francis, James and Maurice Wilkins received the Nobel Prize in Medicine.

1967   Francis published his book, *Of Molecules and Men*.

1969   He took part in the 100th year celebrations of the scientific journal, *Nature*. He also wrote about the future of science in *Nature*.

1972   The Royal Society, an important organization of scientists, presented Francis with the Copley <u>Medal</u>. He received the same award in 1975.

1976   Francis went to do research at the Salk Institute for Biological Studies in California.

1977   He moved permanently to California.

1981   Francis began to concentrate on neuroscience instead of molecular biology. He published his book, *Life Itself: Its Origin and Nature*. Other scientific publications followed over the next years.

1988   Francis published the story of his life, *What Mad Pursuit: A Personal View of Scientific Discovery.*

1991   Francis was given the Order of Merit by Queen Elizabeth II.

2003   He signed the *Humanist Manifesto*, along with 20 other Nobel Prize winners. The Francis Crick Lecture was started, an annual prize lecture for young scientists.

2004   Francis died, aged 88, in San Diego, California, USA.

◆ Glossary ◆

acid VARIABLE NOUN
An **acid** is a liquid or other substance with a pH value of less than 7. Strong **acids** can damage your skin and clothes.

acknowledge TRANSITIVE VERB
If someone's achievements or qualities **are acknowledged**, they are known about and accepted by a lot of people, or by a particular group of people.

administration UNCOUNTABLE NOUN
Administration is the range of activities connected with organizing the way that an organization works and making sure this happens properly.

anaesthetic VARIABLE NOUN
Anaesthetic is a sort of medicine that stops you feeling pain during an operation.

appoint TRANSITIVE VERB
If someone **is appointed to** an important job, they are given that job.

apprentice TRANSITIVE VERB
To **be apprenticed to** someone means to work for them in order to learn the special skill that they have.

aristocrat COUNTABLE NOUN
An **aristocrat** is someone whose family is very important in society.

astronomy UNCOUNTABLE NOUN
Astronomy is the scientific study of the stars, planets, and other natural objects in space.

Bachelor of Arts SINGULAR NOUN
A **Bachelor of Arts** is a first degree from a university in an arts subject such as history or literature.

Bachelor of Science SINGULAR NOUN
A **Bachelor of Science** is a first degree from a university in a science subject.

baronet COUNTABLE NOUN
In Britain, a **baronet** is a man who has been given the title 'Sir' by the king or queen, or who has the title because his father had it before him. In the past, **baronets** were members of the House of Lords

beehive COUNTABLE NOUN
A **beehive** is a sort of box in which bees are kept, which is designed so that the person who looks after them can collect the honey that they produce.

beetle COUNTABLE NOUN
A **beetle** is an insect with a hard cover to its body.

botanist COUNTABLE NOUN
A **botanist** is a scientist who studies plants.

botany UNCOUNTABLE NOUN
Botany is the scientific study of plants.

breed (breeds, breeding, bred)
TRANSITIVE VERB
If you **breed** animals or plants, you keep them for the purpose of producing more animals or plants.

cell COUNTABLE NOUN
A **cell** is the smallest part of an animal or plant. Animals and plants are made up of millions of **cells**.

coal miner COUNTABLE NOUN
A **coal miner** is a person whose job is to work underground and dig out coal.

commissioner COUNTABLE NOUN
A **commissioner** is an important person in a commission, which is a government organization responsible for controlling a particular activity.

convent COUNTABLE NOUN
A **convent** is a sort of church in which religious women live.

convict TRANSITIVE VERB
If someone **is convicted of** a crime, they are found guilty of it in a law court.

Count COUNTABLE NOUN,
TITLE NOUN
A **Count** is a male member of a family that is very important in society.

cross-breed (cross-breeds, cross-breeding, cross-bred)
VERB
If you **cross-breed** plants, you use two different sorts together to produce a new sort.

curved ADJECTIVE
A **curved** object has the shape of a curve or has a smoothly bending surface.

demonstration COUNTABLE NOUN
A **demonstration** of something is a talk by someone who shows you how to do it or how it works.

DNA UNCOUNTABLE NOUN
DNA is something that is contained in the cells of all living things. It is responsible for the way every cell is made and for what every cell does. **DNA** is an abbreviation for 'deoxyribonucleic acid'.

DNA fingerprinting
UNCOUNTABLE NOUN
DNA fingerprinting is a method scientists use to say exactly who someone is by analysing a tiny piece of their skin, hair, etc.

electrolysis UNCOUNTABLE NOUN
Electrolysis is the process of pushing electricity through a liquid in order to make chemical changes in it.

element COUNTABLE NOUN
An **element** is a substance such as gold, oxygen, or carbon that consists of only one type of atom.

emperor COUNTABLE NOUN
An **emperor** is a man who rules an empire, which is a group of countries.

faculty COUNTABLE NOUN
In some universities, a **faculty** is a group of departments that deal with similar subjects.

forensic ADJECTIVE
Forensic scientists carry out scientific examinations of objects in order to discover information about a crime.

fossil COUNTABLE NOUN
Fossils are the dead bodies of creatures that lived millions of years ago, often found in rock.

founder COUNTABLE NOUN
The **founder** of a branch of science is the first person to study it and make it known.

gauze UNCOUNTABLE NOUN
Gauze is a type of thin light material with tiny holes in it.

gene COUNTABLE NOUN
A **gene** is the part of a cell in a living thing which controls the way it will develop.

genetic ADJECTIVE
You use **genetic** to describe something that is concerned with genetics or with genes.

genetics UNCOUNTABLE NOUN
Genetics is the study of how genes control the development of living things.

germ COUNTABLE NOUN
A **germ** is a living thing that you cannot see because it is so small. **Germs** can give people a disease.

guillotine COUNTABLE NOUN
A **guillotine** is a piece of equipment used to kill people as a punishment. It has a heavy, sharp metal blade which drops onto the person's neck. **Guillotines** were used in the past in France, especially during the French Revolution.

gunpowder UNCOUNTABLE NOUN
Gunpowder is a powder which is used to make fireworks and which can make things explode.

helix COUNTABLE NOUN
A **helix** is a shape that is made from one line that bends round and round. In a **double helix**, two lines bend round each other.

heredity UNCOUNTABLE NOUN
Heredity is the biological process by which children get their characteristics from their parents.

HMS NOUN
HMS is used before the names of ships in the British Royal Navy. **HMS** is an abbreviation for 'Her Majesty's Ship' or 'His Majesty's Ship'.

honour COUNTABLE NOUN
An **honour** is a special prize given to someone by the ruler or government of their country because they have done something very good in their life.

with great honours PHRASE
If you leave a university **with great honours**, it means you got very good marks.

infected ADJECTIVE
An **infected** animal is one that has a disease which it can pass to other animals or to people.

infection COUNTABLE NOUN
An **infection** is a disease that can go from one person to another, or from animals to people.

inject TRANSITIVE VERB
To **inject** someone **with** a liquid such as a medicine, or to **inject** it **into** them, means to push it into their body using a needle.

inspire TRANSITIVE VERB
If someone **inspires** you, they give you new ideas and make you want to start doing a particular activity.

journal COUNTABLE NOUN
A **journal** is a serious magazine that deals with a particular subject in a lot of detail.

medal COUNTABLE NOUN
A **medal** is a small metal disc that is given as a special prize by a government or important organization to someone who has done very good work in a particular activity such as science or literature.

molecular biology UNCOUNTABLE NOUN
Molecular biology is the scientific study of the complex chemicals that are found in living things.

monastery COUNTABLE NOUN
A monastery is a sort of church in which religious men live.

monk COUNTABLE NOUN
A **monk** is a religious man who lives with other religious men in a special community.

natural history UNCOUNTABLE NOUN
Natural history is the study of animals and plants and other living things.

naturalist COUNTABLE NOUN
A **naturalist** is a person who studies animals, plants, and other living things.

neuroscience UNCOUNTABLE NOUN
Neuroscience is the scientific study of the way in which the brain is connected to the rest of the body, and how it sends and receives information about feeling, light, movement etc.

Nobel Prize COUNTABLE NOUN
A **Nobel Prize** is one of a set of prizes that are awarded each year to people who have done important work in science, literature, or economics, or for world peace.

origin VARIABLE NOUN
You can refer to the beginning of something, or the reason it started, as its **origin** or its **origins**.

paper COUNTABLE NOUN
A **paper** is a serious piece of writing about a scientific subject which says something new about the subject.

peasant COUNTABLE NOUN
In the past, **peasants** were poor people who worked on the land and not in towns or cities.

PhD COUNTABLE NOUN
A **PhD** is a degree awarded to people who have done advanced research. **PhD** is an abbreviation for 'Doctor of Philosophy'.

ratio COUNTABLE NOUN
A **ratio** is a description of two amounts or quantities which says how much bigger one amount or quantity is than the other one.

release TRANSITIVE VERB
1 To **release** someone who has been kept in prison means to let them leave.

2 When a liquid, gas, or a form of energy such as light or sound **is released** from something, it escapes from it.

reproduce TRANSITIVE VERB, INTRANSITIVE VERB
When people, animals, or plants **reproduce**, they produce more of themselves.

revenge UNCOUNTABLE NOUN
Revenge involves hurting someone on purpose because they have hurt you.

Reverend TITLE NOUN
Reverend is used before the name of some priests in the Christian religion.

revolution VARIABLE NOUN
A **revolution** is a successful attempt by a large group of people to change the government of their country using force.

revolutionary COUNTABLE NOUN
A **revolutionary** is a person who tries to cause a revolution or who takes part in one.

saliva UNCOUNTABLE NOUN
Saliva is a liquid that is like water, which forms naturally in your mouth.

seasick ADJECTIVE
If someone is **seasick** when they are in a boat, they feel sick or they are sick because of the way the boat is moving.

seed VARIABLE NOUN
A **seed** is one of the small hard parts of a plant from which a new plant grows.

sentence TRANSITIVE VERB
When someone **is sentenced** in a court of law, the judge tells them what their punishment will be.

silkworm COUNTABLE NOUN
A **silkworm** is the young form of a sort of Chinese butterfly which produces silk.

slavery UNCOUNTABLE NOUN
Slavery is a system in which some people are owned by other people, and are forced to work for them.

species COUNTABLE NOUN
A **species** is a group of plants or animals of the same type.

specimen COUNTABLE NOUN
A **specimen** is an example or small amount of something which gives an idea of what they are all like or what the whole thing is like.

spiral ADJECTIVE
A **spiral** shape winds round and round, with each curve above or outside the previous one.

statistical ADJECTIVE
Statistical methods involve finding out facts about something by examining numbers and measurements that are known about it.

sting TRANSITIVE VERB
If a bee **stings** you, it pushes something sharp into your skin so that you feel a hot pain.

structure VARIABLE NOUN
The **structure of** something is the way in which all its parts fit together.

substance COUNTABLE NOUN
A **substance** is something that you can touch, like a solid or a liquid, or that you can smell or feel, like a gas.

surgeon COUNTABLE NOUN
A **surgeon** is a doctor who does operations on people to remove or repair an unhealthy part of their body.

taxidermy UNCOUNTABLE NOUN
Taxidermy is the activity of filling the skins of dead animals/ birds with a special material to make them look as if they are alive.

theology UNCOUNTABLE NOUN
Theology is the study of religion and the nature of God.

tobacco UNCOUNTABLE NOUN
Tobacco is the dried leaves of a plant which people smoke in pipes, cigars, and cigarettes.

tortoise COUNTABLE NOUN
A **tortoise** is a slow-moving animal with a hard outer cover into which it can pull its head and legs for protection.

tragically ADVERB
If something happens **tragically**, it is extremely sad, usually because it involves death or extreme pain.

trait COUNTABLE NOUN
A **trait** is a particular characteristic or quality that someone or something has that makes them different from others of the same sort.

twist TRANSITIVE VERB
If you **twist** something, you turn it to make a spiral shape, for example by turning the two ends of it in opposite directions.

unique ADJECTIVE
If something is **unique**, nothing else exists that is exactly the same as it.

unveil TRANSITIVE VERB
If someone **unveils** something such as a new statue or painting, they draw back the curtain which is covering it, in a special ceremony.

vaccine VARIABLE NOUN
A **vaccine** is a substance that is a harmless form of a disease. It is given to people to stop them from getting that disease.

widow COUNTABLE NOUN
A **widow** is a woman whose husband has died.

wrinkled ADJECTIVE
A surface that is **wrinkled** is not smooth but has a lot of lines on it, like the skin on the face of a very old person.

Collins
English Readers

THE AMAZING PEOPLE READERS SERIES:

Level 1

Amazing Inventors
978-0-00-754494-3

Amazing Leaders
978-0-00-754492-9

Amazing Entrepreneurs and Business People
978-0-00-754501-8

Amazing Women
978-0-00-754493-6

Amazing Performers
978-0-00-754508-7

Level 2

Amazing Aviators
978-0-00-754495-0

Amazing Architects and Artists
978-0-00-754496-7

Amazing Composers
978-0-00-754502-5

Amazing Mathematicians
978-0-00-754503-2

Amazing Medical People
978-0-00-754509-4

Level 3

Amazing Explorers
978-0-00-754497-4

Amazing Writers
978-0-00-754498-1

Amazing Philanthropists
978-0-00-754504-9

Amazing Performers
978-0-00-754505-6

Amazing Scientists
978-0-00-754510-0

Level 4

Amazing Thinkers and Humanitarians
978-0-00-754499-8

Amazing Scientists
978-0-00-754500-1

Amazing Writers
978-0-00-754506-3

Amazing Leaders
978-0-00-754507-0

Amazing Entrepreneurs and Business People
978-0-00-754511-7

Visit **www.collinselt.com/readers** for language activities, teacher's notes, and to find out more about the series.